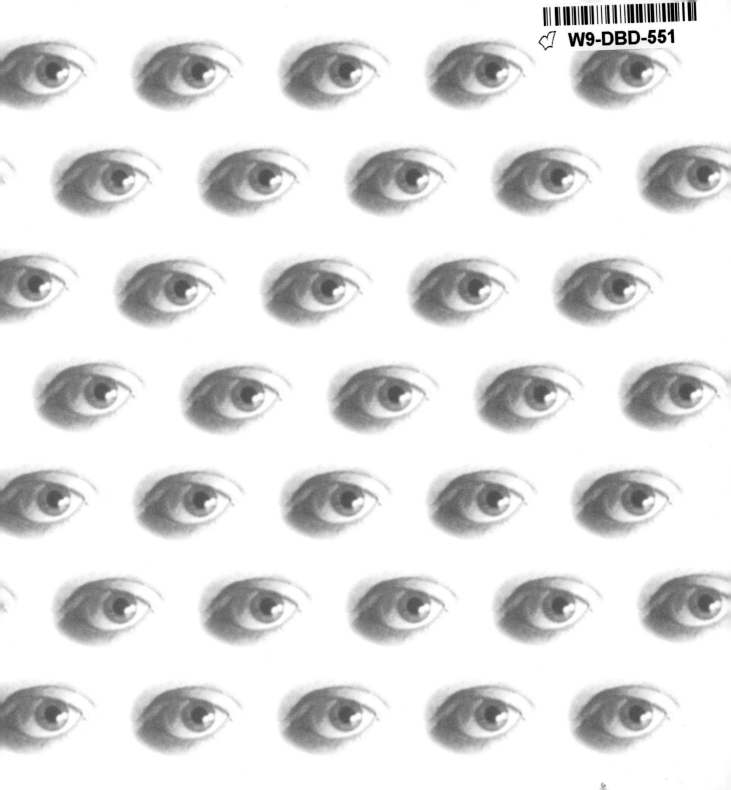

PHILIPPE STARCK

FAY SWEET

PHILIPPE STARCK

Subverchic Design

WATSON-GUPTILL
PUBLICATIONS
New York

First published in 1999 in the United States of America
by Watson-Guptill Publications, a division of
BPI Communications, Inc.,
1515 Broadway, New York, NY 10036

Library of Congress Catalog Card Number: 98-86822

ISBN 0-8230-1200-X

This book was conceived,
designed, and produced by
THE IVY PRESS LTD
2/3 St. Andrews Place
Lewes
East Sussex BN7 1UP

Art Director: Terry Jeavons
Design and page layout: Harry Green
Commissioning Editor: Christine Davis
Editorial Director: Sophie Collins

Originated and printed by Hong Kong Graphic, Hong Kong

Contents

Philippe Starck is never short of surprises. The latest is his proclamation that he will soon stop designing. Coming from someone who is arguably the most famous designer on the planet, this is startling news indeed. His oeuvre is spectacularly impressive, embracing hundreds of designs—among the most familiar are the curious three-legged aluminum lemon squeezer, the cute Miss Sissy lamps, the Café Costes chair, the horn-shaped Ara desk lamp, and, of course, the elegant plastic toothbrush. And then there are the incredibly popular Royalton and Paramount hotels in New York, and the dozens of other interior projects around the world. Now that he has reached the age of 50 and the world enters a new millennium, he feels it is time for change. It is a time for assessment, for considering how we can best use our knowledge and resources to significantly improve our lot. He believes we must rise above our barbaric tendencies and aspire to become more compassionate, more considerate, more loving. ★ In his last phase as a designer he has concentrated his energies on one final, massive, innovative global project: a new range of utility products embracing everything from clothes and furniture to music and organic foods. It is Starck's gift to the planet. He believes his job is to repair and to put back something. Called "Good Goods," the first products came on the market in autumn 1998. ★ In the final months of a career that in 20 years has catapulted him to megastar status,

Starck continues to work at his usual frenetic pace. His trademark disheveled look—crumpled black T-shirt and jeans, and omnipresent stubble—has altered slightly: he's much slimmer since becoming a vegetarian on the birth of his son in 1996. He's a restless presence, humming and singing his way through every day as he scribbles down sketches and notes on the tracing-paper jotter pad that's always close at hand. Juggling at least two hundred projects—from a new fly swatter to a trio of hotels in London—he rarely stays in one place for long. Starck's designs are usually born in the creative solitude of any one of his dozen homes, but he regularly visits his Paris studio to check on his "tribe" of design, marketing, and organizing staff. Here, inside the pistachio-green building—designed by Starck—on an island in the Seine, the office is buzzing, prototypes and completed designs stacked high on trestle tables. Awaiting Starck's arrival there's a pile of letters to be answered, lists of questions about current projects, and a line of people waiting for meetings that are always running late. When not in France, he's visiting sites, factories, and clients in Japan, Germany, Italy, and England. ★ Starck says he has no idea what he might do when all this stops: "I will be free and open to something new; maybe I'll just disappear." This being Starck, expect the unexpected. ★ **Fay Sweet**

You are predicting big changes to the way we live in the new millennium. What do you see happening? The year 2000 is a very symbolic date. It means nothing, but marks a moment when we can stop and think about our lives, about society today, about the world in which we live. Are we happy or not? Do we like what we see, or can we recognize that society may need some improvements? This interests me very much. I think we need to make some changes for the better, but I find it curious that our politicians are so very quiet—where are their ideas for our future, where are the suggestions for improving lives? If these so-called leaders are saying nothing, then I think we should all say what we think. My contribution is to make certain proposals. Obviously I am not a politician, a philosopher, a sociologist, a singer, I am just a Christmas gift designer, but I believe that everyone can and should propose something. My proposals are made based on what I know, and use what few skills I have. At the center of my collection of ideas is the knowledge that we are entering a phase where we will want to shed the excesses of the past ten to fifteen narcissistic years. We need fewer possessions in our lives, and those items that we do own must be better made than before, they must be reduced to the basics, and they must be long-lasting. We can use our huge knowledge of design and technology to make the best and most economic use of materials. We should promote built-in longevity, because this makes a lot more sense than recycling. These Things in our lives musT be ecologically correcT, buT musT also be poliTically and morally correcT. I suggesT ThaT These new producTs be made wiTh consideraTion for The planeT, by people who are paid a fair wage, and wiThouT The involvemenT of greedy profiT-makers. **How does your new Good Goods range of products reflect your latest ideas?** The Good Goods caTalog is The culminaTion of years of ThoughT and ideas. IT will Take several years To see everyThing come To fruiTion. The full TiTle is "Good Goods by STarck: The CaTalog of Non-ProducTs for The Non-Consumer for The NexT Moral MarkeT." The name Good Goods was coined by The greaT American designer Charles Eames, who was The besT and mosT moral designer. IT is a global proposal, my lasT major work, and iT is abouT The equipmenT of life—abouT food, washing powder, cloThes, music, books, TransporTaTion, furniTure, Toys. I call These The "No ProducTs." They are No ProducTs because They are noT creaTed by markeTing or adverTising or by greedy people wanTing To make piles of money; These are The basics of life made To fulfill a funcTion wiTh respecT, fanTasy, creaTiviTy, Tenderness, humor, and love. AT The sTudio we have operaTed a moral policy for many years: we do noT work for religion, weapons manufacTurers, alcohol producers, Tobacco companies—in facT, anyone who makes dirTy money. More recenTly we have sTopped using anyThing which causes deaTh—so we no longer use leaTher. This laTesT projecT is an exTension of This philosophy. Using all our knowledge, No ProducTs incorporaTe

The best possible designs, using the minimum of materials. The materials must have sound ecological credentials; the products are made by people who are paid a fair wage, and they are sold at a fair price. We are working with very big names here, with Alessi and Virgin, for example. Because this is a new idea, it is not possible to make it fit with old systems, so the products will not be sold in shops. Shops are part of the old way, they're obsolete; they involve lots of travel, they are not accessible to everybody, and they are expensive because they must make plenty of money for the landlord. Good Goods will be sold through a mail-order catalog and via the Internet—this is a way people like to shop, it is elegant, and it will become increasingly popular. My key word here is 'subverchic' —I want to be subversive in a chic way. No products are created for the invisible tribe I call The Non-Consumer, people who don't need so many things in their life, who want simplicity. I think that today people are suspicious of the marketplace. We are tired of being considered open-mouthed, stupid animals. We are tired of venal advertising and we are tired of being offered products which are created just for profit. I think this must change, and we must make humanity the priority, not materialism. For decades we have lived a lie, believing that all these products have been created to serve us and provide a better life. But this is simply untrue: we have come to serve the products, and life is no better. The initial idea wasn't a bad one, but it has now become warped. It's time

To redefine The Targets. With my new proposals we put people first. It is The people who profit. Of course, what I make is not perfect; it is a proposal and you can either agree with it or not. The idea is That it is a criticism of what exists, and is a step Toward a better life. I want The Good Goods To prime The pump. This is The first Trickle of ideas, and I hope There will be a flood of many, many more. Good Goods will show The way Toward a new relationship between The producer and The consumer, and between products and The consumer. I hope people will understand what I am Trying To do and That others will follow with Their own ideas. **Isn't yours quite a hard act to follow?** There's plenty of room for others in many different areas. For example, I'm also involved in a range of organic foods. I want everyone To become a vegetarian. This is going To be a very hard Task because it involves altruism, and people are basically not altruistic. My strategy is To attract Them To The idea Through really excellent organic food and Then push Them slowly Toward being vegetarian. I became a vegetarian a few years ago at The birth of my son Oa. I had been Thinking about it for a very long Time, but my son's birth was a vital moment. I didn't want him To be eaten by animals, so I could see no reason for us To eat The children of animals. Becoming vegetarian is very important for me because if we humans insist on saying That we are different from animals and That we are not barbarians, Then we should stop killing. It is impossible To be civilized if we continue To kill. **So how does your recent design for a fly swatter for Alessi fit into this picture?** I am noT a purisT. IT is jusT a small Thing, noThing. IT brings some poeTry To a banal objecT. We can allow ourselves a liTTle fanTasy. However, I do have some bad feelings abouT IT now. I'm no longer happy To kill flies. BuT IT is a piece of fanTasy. IT is also very effecTive and IT is ecological because IT's a greaT deal kinder To The planeT Than chemical spray. IT's been so successful, IT's been selling like a bomb—ThaT's why we call IT Dr. Skud. **Is the Good Goods range a rejection of fashion?** I'm noT againsT fashion, buT I do Think ThaT Today There is compliciTy beTween The consumer and fashion producers of all sorTs. There is noThing beTTer Than a new fashion To make someThing obsoleTe, and so The wheels jusT keep Turning. This is wasTeful. IT is noT moral. I am suggesTing a new way of Thinking based on The idea of The classic liTTle black dress. Many of us wanT jusT a few good, well-made basic possessions; To dress Them up and make Them exciTing we can add inTeresTing accessories. This gives us The opporTuniTy To make The besT use of The world's resources while also having some fanTasy and fun. I esTimaTe ThaT many people Today will find ThaT 95 percenT of Their wardrobe is fashion-based, wiTh jusT five percenT being basic essenTials. I suggesT ThaT someThing like 25 percenT should be fashion, and 75 percenT basic essenTials. This will reduce The amounT of obsolescence and Therefore wasTe. **Do you think ordinary people will be interested in rejecting materialism?**

I Think many, many people are ready To casT ofF Their excess baggage. I can'T undersTand people who collecT Things. OF course IT will Take Time for everyone To see This new way. BuT I Think in 50 years we will see a really big diFFerence. Every age has iTs period of reflecTion, and This is ours. OF course we couldn'T ask The young To be reflecTive, because They are egoTisTical and need To express Themselves. The problem comes when you conTinue To be egoTisTical in The second half of your life. I was egoTisTical when I was young, so now iT's Time for me To be ThoughTFul. **Isn't it a luxury of the rich and comfortable to say that they need very few things to exist?** ThaT is True—of course The hungry have no need To dieT—buT IT will change. EvenTually everyone will come To see ThaT less really is more. Life can be more serene. We can all beneFiT if we all consume less. OF course The idea will Take longer To Flower in some places Than oThers. I am so sad when I see poor counTries Trying To produce so much; I always hope They will noT make The same misTakes as us, buT They do. We can only hope ThaT They do iT more quickly and go Through The maTerial phase FasTer. I am an opTimisT and believe Things will improve. UnTil jusT a few years ago I was a pessimisT. IT Took me a long Time To realize ThaT pessimism was sTupid and useless. As an opTimisT, I can be acTively working on soluTions insTead of wasTing energy feeling bad abouT The problems. I have faiTh in people, buT There are always plenTy of Things To change. For example, I believe we should all take responsibility for ourselves. I want people to understand there is no such thing as pardon. The worst mechanism ever invented is the idea that a prayer or confession will result in pardon. This is rubbish—we are all responsible for everything we do. But I don't know how we can make such a change—my job is not to enforce, but to propose.

Is your latest project a reaction against the excesses of the 1980s? Life has its natural cycles. I believe that society travels through light and shadows. We are emerging from a long period of light and entering a cycle of shadow. By doing this we are leaving a period of great luxury where we have been able to amuse ourselves for ten to fifteen years doing small, naughty things. But now the time has come for war, to engage in the battle of fighting off the barbarian. We want to work on something I call "l'homme sublime." The idea here is that, with care, and if we keep the barbarian within us at bay, humans can now enjoy a return on the investment of past civilizations. We should learn everything we can from the past to make sure there is no more hunger and illness. Then we can head toward perfection. **Do you have any regrets about the 1980s?** I have regrets about everything I do. I don't like what I do, even what I am, that's why I'm driven to do something else and make it better. Today that means less. I try to apply the same philosophy to myself, to make myself better. For example, I recently undertook a two-week fast. This was a very interesting experiment for someone like me—I've eaten and drunk well all my life. However, it was fascinating. By eating less you become very clear, you discover reality and feel so much better in the body and in the head. Everybody must do this. Less is more. In the past five years I have changed completely. I am not the same man—now I am far more well tuned. Our civilization is based on the idea of making progress, so I cannot stop—I have to make things better, it is poetic. It is not enough to make things of beauty, however; they must also be good. The beautiful object was the product of a particular cultural regime, a regime obsessed with aesthetics. The problem with this is that the regime was ruled by the laws of taste, by what is in fashion and what is out of fashion. These laws are some of the most important levers of consumerism and lead to over-consumption. Now we are about to realize that aesthetics alone are not enough; in fact, they are dangerous, unsatisfying, insubstantial. But we will always need products, so a new way must be developed to make them. If we had to, we could clean a toilet with a branch off a tree or an old brush—but we prefer something perhaps a little more interesting. A good object, I think, not only does the job, but also contains some humor and love. A good object renders its service with grace. This is much more sophisticated than relying only on aesthetics. **When you are designing, do you know instantly if the idea is a good one?** Yes. I have very good intuition and a very good feeling for rhythms. **Have you ever been wrong?** All the time.

STARCK

ON THE OBJECT

We will always need products, but I believe we should think about them in a new and different way. I have now rationalized my approach to designing products and bring the same set of values to bear whether I'm designing a car, a toothbrush, or a waste-processing plant. Not only is it necessary to design within certain moral and ecological parameters, but also we can make objects that really help us to progress as a civilization. Objects can be used to criticize society, to provoke debate. For me, the real success of a design is when it starts a conversation between two people. I think it's also possible to use objects to encourage us to be more compassionate. For too long the mechanical objects in our everyday lives, the cars and bikes, for example, have been designed as macho symbols; they are very aggressive. My idea is to sexually reposition these things and make them female. As for materials, the future is synthetic, synthetic, synthetic. This way we don't have to cut down trees or kill cows. Synthetic materials are absolutely the best things we can make use of today. The key is to work with a good moral producer, someone who knows how to handle the materials ecologically. The functional reason is clear. The poetic reason for using synthetic materials is that they are a product of human intelligence and that makes them extremely beautiful. I love human intelligence. I am an aficionado. In addition to synthetics, we make use of really good, moral and ecological materials. Our 'Bio'cotton is organically grown, and 'Eco' is free of all chemical treatments.

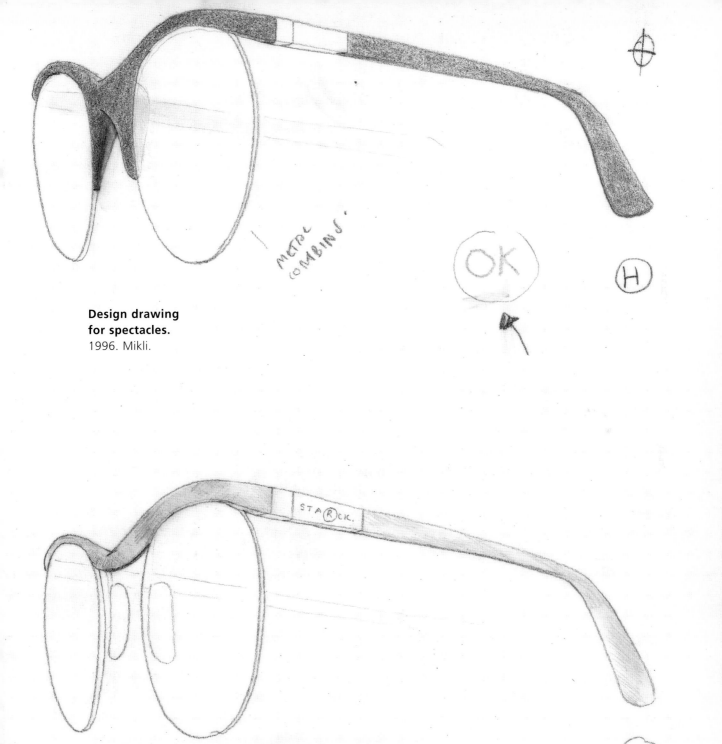

**Design drawing
for spectacles.**
1996. Mikli.

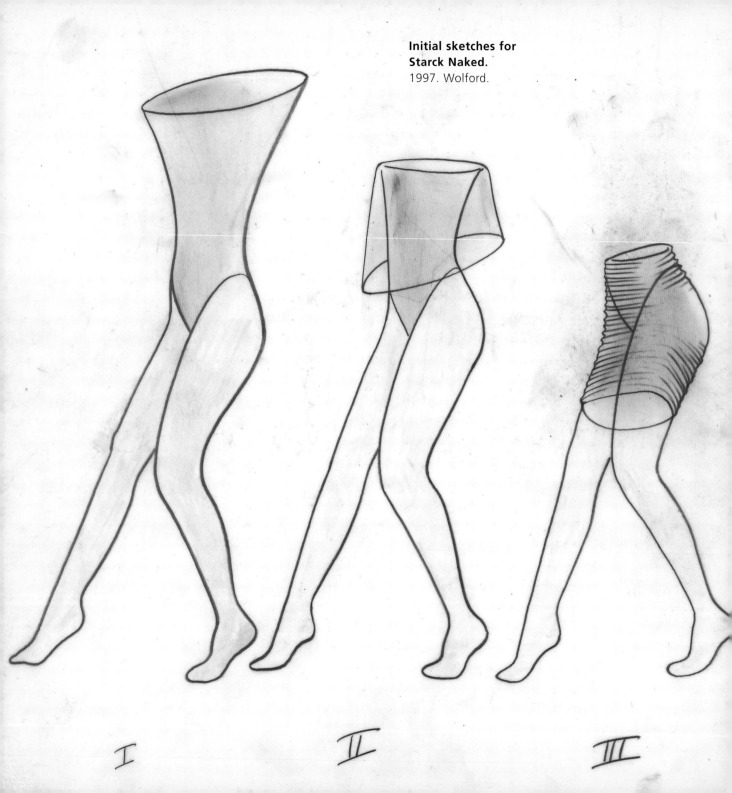

I

II

III

NOUS
SOMMES

NOUS NOUS NOUS NOUS NO   NOUS NOUS N   US NOUS NOUS NOUS NOUS NO   OUS NOUS NO   S NOUS NOUS
NOUS NOUS NOUS NOUS NOUS N   NOUS NOUS N   US NOUS NOUS NOUS NOUS NO   OUS NOUS NO   S NOUS NOUS
NOUS NOUS NOUS NOUS NOUS NO   NOUS NOUS N   US NOUS NOUS NOUS NOUS NO   OUS NOUS NO   S NOUS NOUS
NOUS NOUS NOUS NOUS NOUS NOU   NOUS NOUS N   US NOUS NOUS NOUS NOUS NO   OUS NOUS NO   S NOUS NOUS
NOUS NOUS N   OUS NOUS NOUS   NOUS NOUS N   US NOUS NOU   OUS NOUS NO   S NOUS NOUS
NOUS NOUS N   US NOUS NOUS   NOUS NOUS N   US NOUS NOU   OUS NOUS NO   S NOUS NOUS
NOUS NOUS N   S NOUS NOUS   NOUS NOUS N   US NOUS NOUS NOUS NOUS NO   OUS NOUS NO   S NOUS NOUS
NOUS NOUS N   S NOUS NOUS   NOUS NOUS N   US NOUS NOUS NOUS NOUS NO   OUS NOUS NO   S NOUS NOUS
NOUS NOUS N   S NOUS NOUS   NOUS NOUS N   US NOUS NOUS NOUS NOUS NO   OUS NOUS NO   S NOUS NOUS
NOUS NOUS N   S NOUS NOUS   NOUS NOUS N   US NOUS NOU   OUS NOUS NO   S NOUS NOUS
NOUS NOUS N   US NOUS NOUS   NOUS NOUS N   US NOUS NOU   OUS NOUS NO   S NOUS NOUS
NOUS NOUS N   OUS NOUS NOU   NOUS NOUS N   US NOUS NOU   OUS NOUS NOU   US NOUS NOUS
NOUS NOUS NOUS NOUS NOUS NOU   NOUS NOUS N   US NOUS NOUS NOUS NOUS NO   US NOUS NOUS NOUS NOUS NOU
NOUS NOUS NOUS NOUS NOUS NO   NOUS NOUS N   US NOUS NOUS NOUS NOUS NO   S NOUS NOUS NOUS NOUS NO
NOUS NOUS NOUS NOUS NOUS N   NOUS NOUS N   US NOUS NOUS NOUS NOUS NO   NOUS NOUS NOUS NOUS N
NOUS NOUS NOUS NOUS NO   NOUS NOUS N   US NOUS NOUS NOUS NOUS NO   US NOUS NOUS NO

We are God

DEMAINSERAMOINS

Tomorrow will be less

STARCK

When I design, I am both very slow and very fast. Ideas can take up to 30 years to mature, but when I come to draw them they never take more than three minutes to complete. After that it becomes boring. I always work alone in the middle of nowhere. I have a collection of secret places, including my homes and my boat. My office is always in my bedroom, and my desk always faces a view of nature. I try to wake up in time for sunrise, and after some cereal for breakfast I work out a little, take a nap, and then start work. Sometimes I have a project to complete; at other times I have something in my head that I want to put on paper. When it is done I send the drawing immediately to the client. When I produce designs for companies like Alessi and Kartell, I think of myself as the friendly internal enemy. I am a David, but I never fight Goliath with punches, I work from the inside. I am a slow, vicious strategist. One of my greatest triumphs was in cutting the price of my chairs; this was a fine strategy. It started with my first successful chair, Café Costes, which sold for around $700. Every two years thereafter, I won the battle to halve the price of the chairs. After Café Costes came Mr. Blob at around $300, followed by Lord Yo at $140 and Dr. No at $100. The latest is La Marie, which sells for around $50. I can stop here, because otherwise there will be no money left for research.

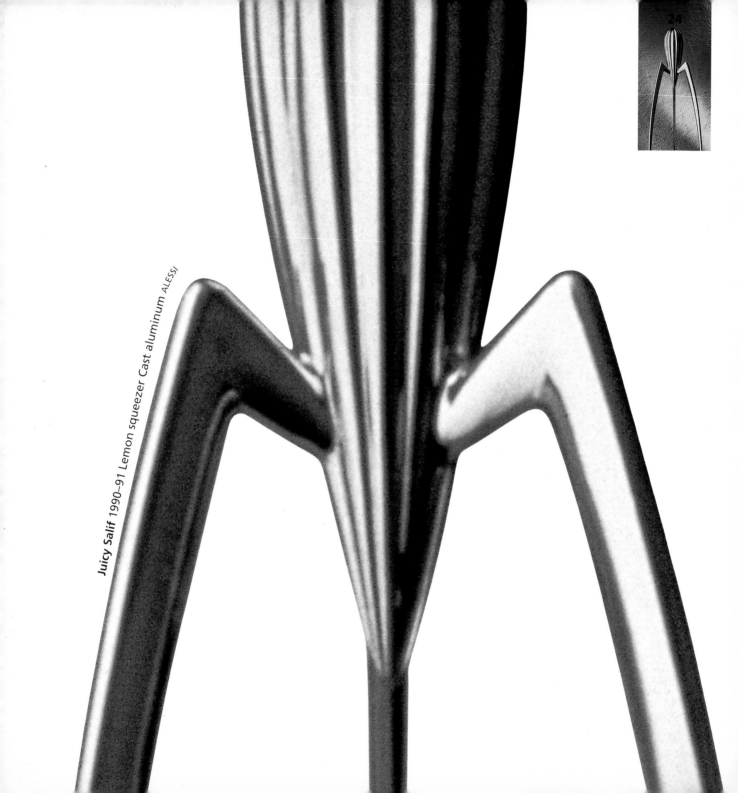

Juicy Salif 1990–91 Lemon squeezer Cast aluminum ALESSI

24

Scooter Lama (prototype) 1992 Motor scooter Plastic recyclable materials APRILIA

Nani Nani 1989 Biomorphic building Tokyo, Japan RIKUGO

27

W W Stool 1990 Stool / Sandblasted cast aluminum VITRA

L'URGENCE EST REVENUE

The sense of urgency is back

LE
CIVISME
EST
D'AVANT
GARDE

To be a good citizen is to be avant-garde

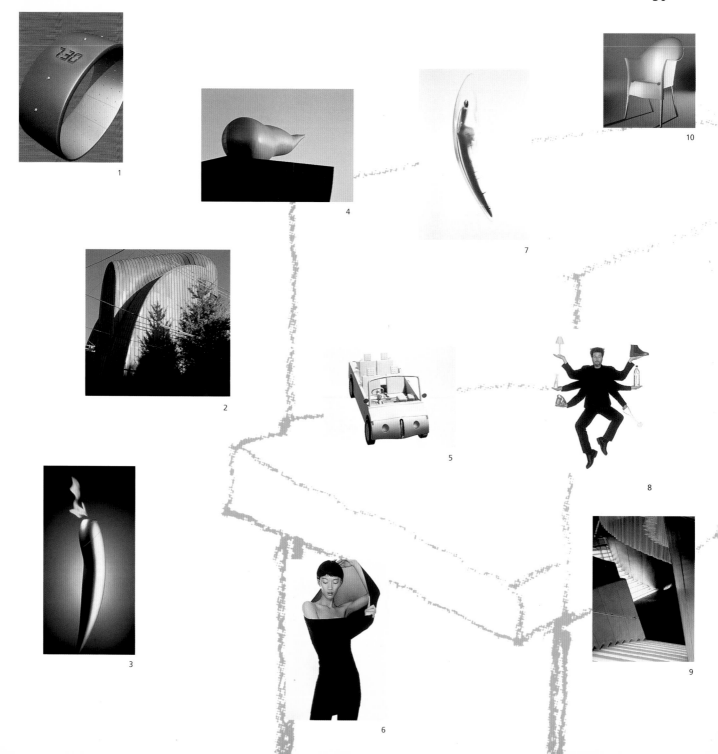

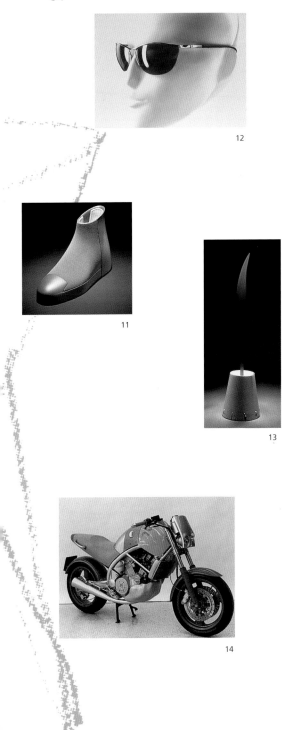

12

11

13

14

15

16

17

1 **Digital Watch (project).** 1989.

2 **Nani Nani.** 1989. Tokyo. Biomorphic building.

3 **Olympic Flame.** 1992. For the Winter Olympics at Albertville, France. Stainless steel.

4 **Asahi Beer Hall.** 1990. Tokyo. Rooftop flame. Asahi Breweries.

5 **Toto la Toto (project).** 1996. Car prototype.

6 **Starck Naked.** 1998. Women's clothing. Wolford.

7 **Alo.** 1996. Voice-command telephone. Concept: Philippe Starck; designer: Jérôme Olivet. Thomson.

8 **Starck as Shiva.** 1998. Featured in Good Goods catalog. La Redoute.

9 **Restaurant Felix.** 1994. Peninsular Hotel, Kowloon, Hong Kong.

10 **Lord Yo.** 1994. Stackable armchair. Polypropylene body, aluminum frame. Driade.

11 **Shoe (prototype).** 1996. Synthetic materials. Della Valle.

12 **Eyeglasses.** 1996. Mikli.

13 **Toothbrush and Holder.** 1989. Fluocaril.

14 **X Ray 1000 (prototype).** 1996. Motorbike. Aprilia.

15 **Boa.** 1996. Stereo FM radio. Concept: Philippe Starck; designer: Claude Bressan. Saba.

16 **Restaurant Teatriz.** 1990. Madrid. Washbasin.

17 **Hook.** 1996. Telephone. ABS plastic. Thomson/Alessi.

Jim Nature 1994 Portable television High-density wood, plastic SABA

Hot Bertaa 1990–91 Kettle Aluminum, plastic ALESSI

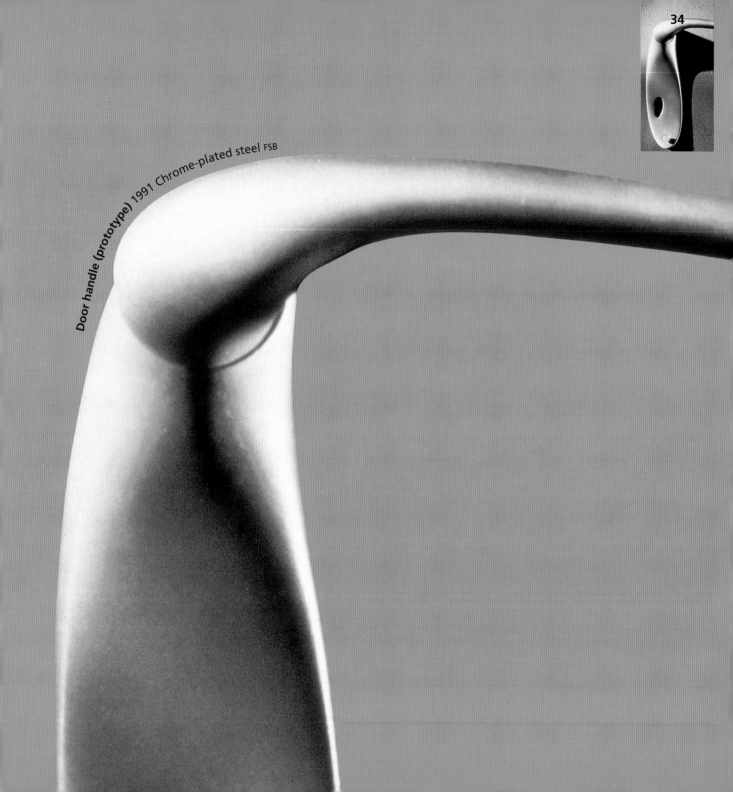

Door handle (prototype) 1991 Chrome-plated steel FSB

34

To Yoo 1996 Telephone ABS plastic THOMSON/ALESSI

Le Moult House
1985–87
Ile St.-Germain, Paris
Private house
Night view

Asahi Beer Hall
1990
Tokyo
Asahi Breweries
Night view

Control Tower
1997
Bordeaux-Merignac
Airport
Competition design

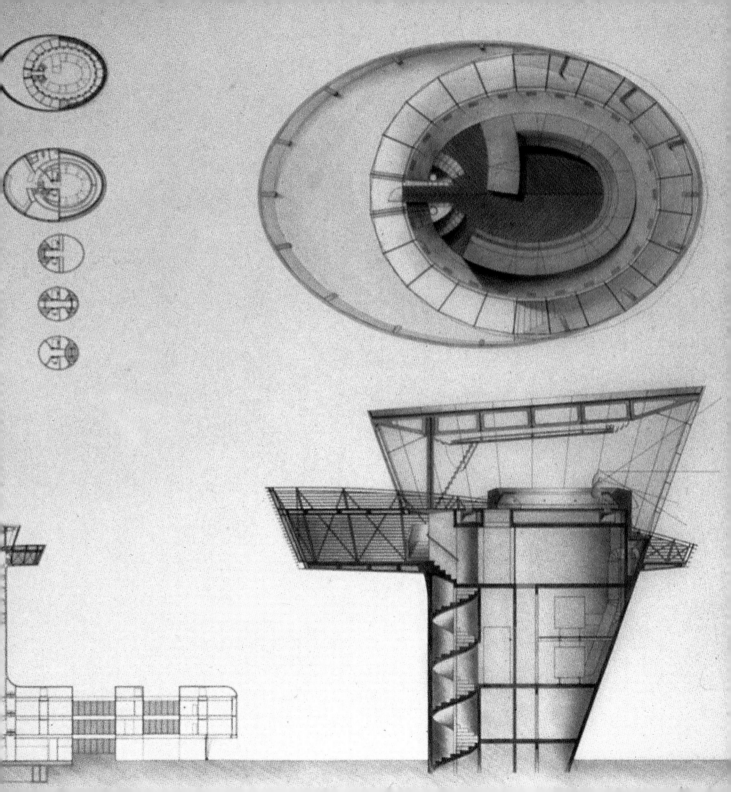

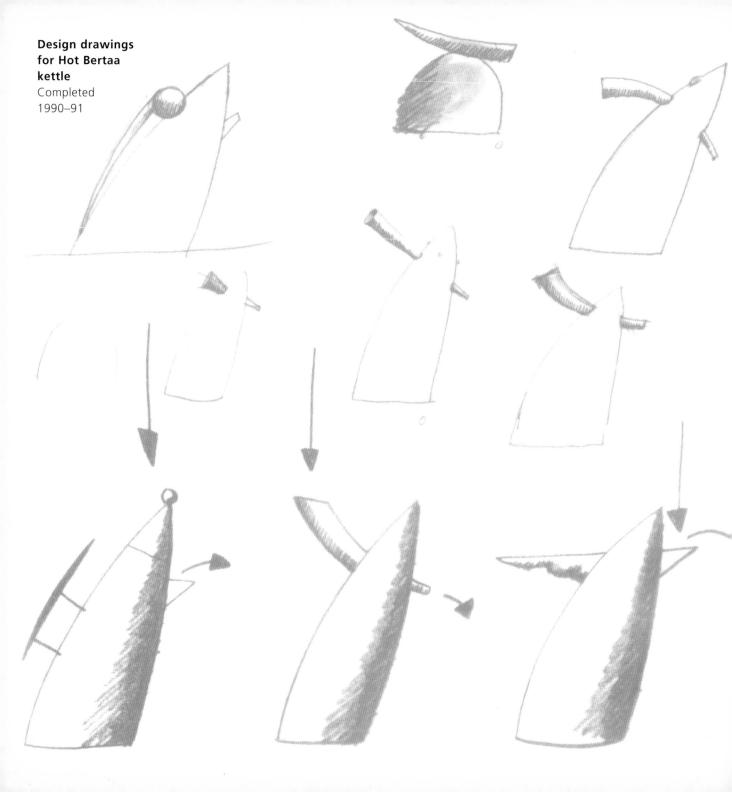

**Design drawings
for Hot Bertaa
kettle**
Completed
1990–91

FACADE SUR LE QUAI JULES-GUESDE ECHELLE 1/500°

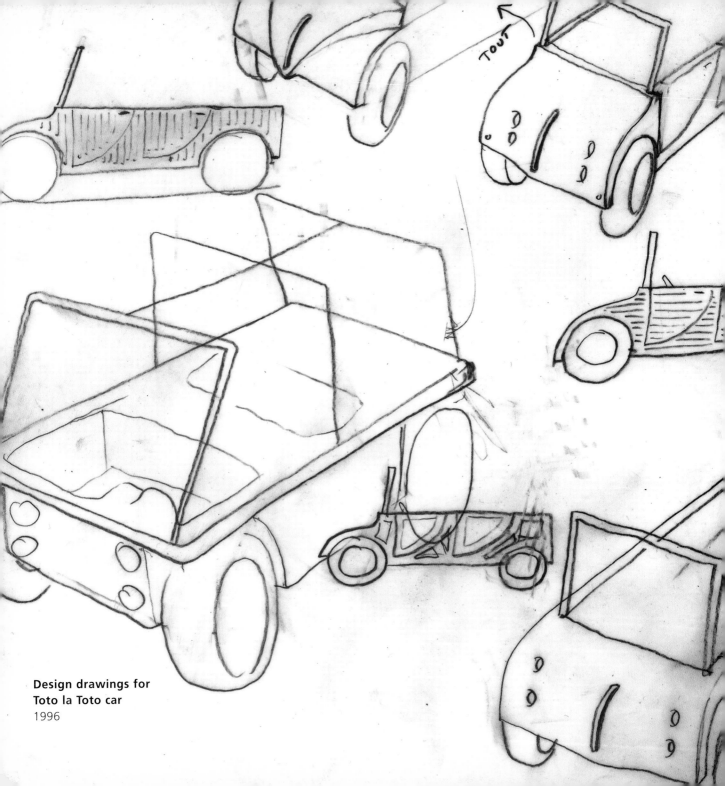

**Design drawings for
Toto la Toto car**
1996

design, manufacture, and purchase of products that are ecologically, politically, and morally sound. These can be all kinds of goods. For example, there's La Marie, perhaps my ultimate chair. Comfortable, stackable, sturdy, uncontrived, and timeless, it is the essential "non-product." There's also a toilet brush called Excalibur, which combines duty with pleasure and an agreeable appearance. In other words, form belies function. On a different level there's G+++, a complex which naturally fortifies, energizes, and stimulates. Indeed, good health in mind and body cannot be underestimated, and so the GoodMusic compilations I've made with Virgin are very important. There's always a tune dancing through my mind, and I'm sure this is one of the most significant influences on my creative work. In assembling these four records, comprising the musical compositions to which I owe the most gratitude, I wanted to convey the various feelings which resonate within all of us at distinct moments in our individual experience. And because we are all now global citizens, I've also included a collection of modern writing. I recommend a story every evening at bedtime, to promote vivid dreams and a pleasant awakening the next morning.

THE FUTURE

L'AMOUR EST UNE ESPECE EN VOIE DE DISPARITION

Love is an endangered species

PARTAGEONS

Let us share together

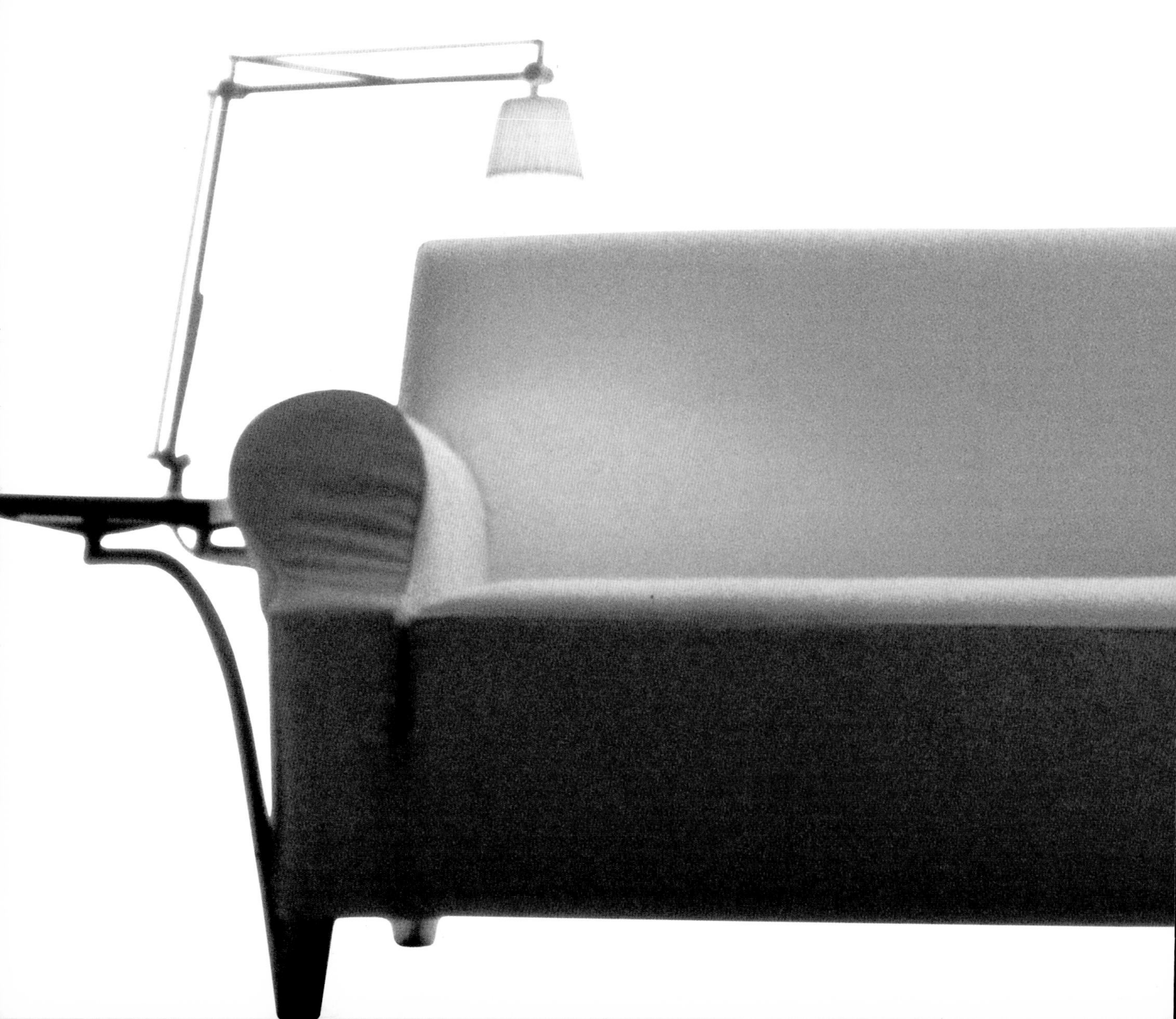

LWS
1998
Lazy working sofa
Foam, cloth,
aluminum, wood
Cassina

Miss COCO
1998
Folding chair
Aluminum, Maderon
Cassina

Archi Moon
1998
Lamp
Aluminum with cloth
or plastic shade
Flos

Dr. Skud
1998
Flyswatter
Polyamide
Alessi

52

GoodMusic
1998
Music compilations corresponding
to different moods and needs
Body, Head, Heart, Conscience
Starck with Virgin

Moto 6,5
1995
Motorbike
Aprilia

Boaat
1998
Storage boxes with convertible
lids for eating/drinking
ABS
Alessi

TeddyBearBand
1998
Children's toy
Synthetic fur
Moulin Roty

Bioderma
1998
Skin-care line
Starck with Bioderma

La gamme **STARCK** with **BIODERMA** est le résultat de la rencontre de deux êtres passionnés. Annie Vinche, à la tête du laboratoire **BIODERMA**, scientifique animée d'un authentique sentiment humaniste ; Philippe Starck, sensible aux mêmes priorités, mais dénué quant à lui de talents dermatologiques. Depuis longtemps utilisateur inconditionnel des produits Bioderma, il a décidé de créer avec Annie Vinche une gamme de soins préventifs essentiels et simples. **ESSENTIELS:** indispensables quotidiennement, sans parfum ajouté qui pourrait dénaturer l'odeur originelle de la peau. **SIMPLES:** d'utilisation aisée, contenant un minimum d'ingrédients, d'une présentation honnête et pratique. Une ligne d'hygiène et de soins quotidiens nécessaires à un mode de vie urbain. L'épiderme est soumis à des agressions multiples - pollution, soleil, vent, froid, chauffage - responsables de la sécheresse qui fragilise la peau et favorise le vieillissement prématuré. Les produits de cette gamme, adaptés à tous les types de peaux et de cheveux, respectent leurs structures et reconstituent le film hydrolipidique qui les protège. Les composants, soigneusement limités en...

STARCK
WITH
BIODERMA
CRÈME
HYDRATANTE

Dr. Cheese
1998
Interdental brush
Thermoplastic resin
Alessi

Excalibur
1995
Toilet brush
Polypropylene with nylon brush
Heller

Le Serpent à Plumes
1998
Fiction anthology in kraft
paper envelope
Book 3, African writers
Le Serpent à Plumes

Dr. Kiss
1998
Toothbrush
Polyamide
Alessi

Eau St. Georges
1997
Mineral water bottle
PET plastic
Eau St. Georges, Corsica

Kayak
1998
Lightweight kayak with "seat on top" design
High-density anti-UV-treated polyethylene
Starck with Rotomod

STARCK

1949 Born in Paris ★ **1965–81** Studies at École Nissim de Camodo, Paris ★ **1968** Sets up first company, producing inflatable objects **1** ★ **1976** Interior design for the Paris nightclub La Main Bleue ★ **1978** Interior design for the Paris nightclub Les Bains Douches ★ **1979** Founds company, Starck Product ★ **1981** Designs Président M table for President Mitterrand's private study in the Élysée Palace ★ **1982** Interior design of Dallas nightclub, Starck Club. Begins designing furniture for the Italian company Driade ★ **1983–84** Refurbishes President Mitterrand's private apartments in the Élysée Palace **2** ★ **1984** Interior design of Café Costes, Paris ★ **1985** Interior design of Café Mystique, Tokyo. Named Chevalier de l'Ordre des Arts et des Lettres ★ **1987** Architecture: Le Moult House (private house), Paris **3** Laguiole cutlery factory, France. Interior design: Manin Restaurant, Tokyo. Other work includes Mandala pasta shape for Panzani **4** ★ **1988** Interior design: Royalton Hotel, New York **5** Café Mystique, Tokyo; La Cigale concert hall, Paris. Other work includes: Lola Mundo table-cum-chair for Driade **6** Ara table lamp for Flos ★ **1989** Architecture: Nani Nani office building, Tokyo. Other work includes: first of several boats for Beneteau; toothbrush for Fluocaril ★ **1990** Architecture: Asahi Beer Hall, Tokyo. Interior design: Paramount Hotel, New York; Restaurant Teatriz, Madrid **7** Other work includes: Juicy Salif lemon squeezer for Alessi; Dr. Glob chair for Kartell ★ **1991** Architecture: École des Beaux-Arts, Paris **8** Interior design: Hugo Boss boutique, Paris

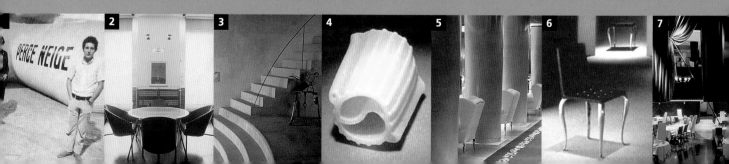

★ **1992** Architecture: Le Baron Vert office block, Osaka, Japan. Interior design: Salon Coppola hairdressing salon, Milan. Other work includes: Louis XX stackable chair for Vitra  Miss Lee energy-saving light for Flos ★ **1993** Interior design: Groningen Museum, the Netherlands. Other work includes: Dadada stool for OWO ★ **1994** Architecture: kit houses for 3 Suisses mail-order catalog Interior design: Felix Restaurant and Oyster Bar, Peninsula Hotel, Hong Kong. Other work includes: Lord Yo stackable armchair for Driade; bathroom furniture for Duravit ★ **1995** Architecture: École Nationale des Arts Décoratifs, Paris; Formentera House (private house), Spain. Interior design: Delano Hotel, Miami Theatron Restaurant, Mexico. Other work includes: Moto 6,5 motorbike for Aprilia; Plasma ultraflat TV for Thomson ★ **1996** Architecture: Placido: Arango Jr. House (private house), Madrid; design for incineration plant at Vitry, France (scheduled for completion 2001) Interior design: Mondrian Hotel, Los Angeles. Other work includes: Dr. No stackable chair for Kartell; Faitoo kitchen utensils for Alessi Oa table lamp for Flos; Alo voice-command telephone for Thomson; eyeglasses for Mikli; Partoo portable TV for Saba ★ **1997** Architecture: air traffic control tower for Bordeaux-Merignac Airport, France ★ **1998** Launches Good Goods mail-order range with La Redoute

CHRONOLOGY

Index

Acknowledgments

The publishers wish to thank Philippe Starck, Anne-Marie Grué and Pierre Doze for their kind assistance with all aspects of this book.

Photographic credits

Contents page, Louis XX chair: photo Vitra/Tom Vack

Page 11, Starck: photo Tom Vack

Page 19, Starck on Dadada stool: photo Tom Vack

Page 23, Starck with Ara lamps: photo Jean-Baptiste Mondino

Page 25, Scooter Lama: photo Gianni Sabbadin

Page 26, Nani Nani: photo T. Waki, Shokokusha

Page 27, WW Stool: photo Vitra/Andreas Sütterlin

Pages 30–31, Digital watch: photo Pascal Cagninacci/DEIS; Olympic flame: photo Hervé Ternisien; Starck Naked: photo Jean-Baptiste Mondino; Alo: photo Guido Mocafico; Starck as Shiva: photo Jean-Baptiste Mondino; Lord Yo: photo Tom Vack; Boa: photo Didier Griffoulière/Edelkoort Conseil; Nani Nani: photo T. Waki, Shokokusha; Hook: photo Hervé Ternisien

Page 32, Jim Nature: photo Jean-François Aloisi

Page 35, To Yoo: photo Hervé Ternisien

Page 36, Asahi Beer Hall: photo Alberto Venzago/Nacása & Partners Inc.

Page 39, Vitry: photos Hervé Ternisien

Page 41, Le Baron Vert: photo Nacása & Partners Inc./Hiroyuki Hirai

Page 43, Philippe Starck: photo Jean-Baptiste Mondino

Pages 60–61, Mandala: photo Hervé Ternisien; Royalton Hotel: photo Tom Vack; Lola Mundo: photo Tom Vack; Louis XX: photo Andreas Sütterlin; Starck house: photo Jacques Dirand

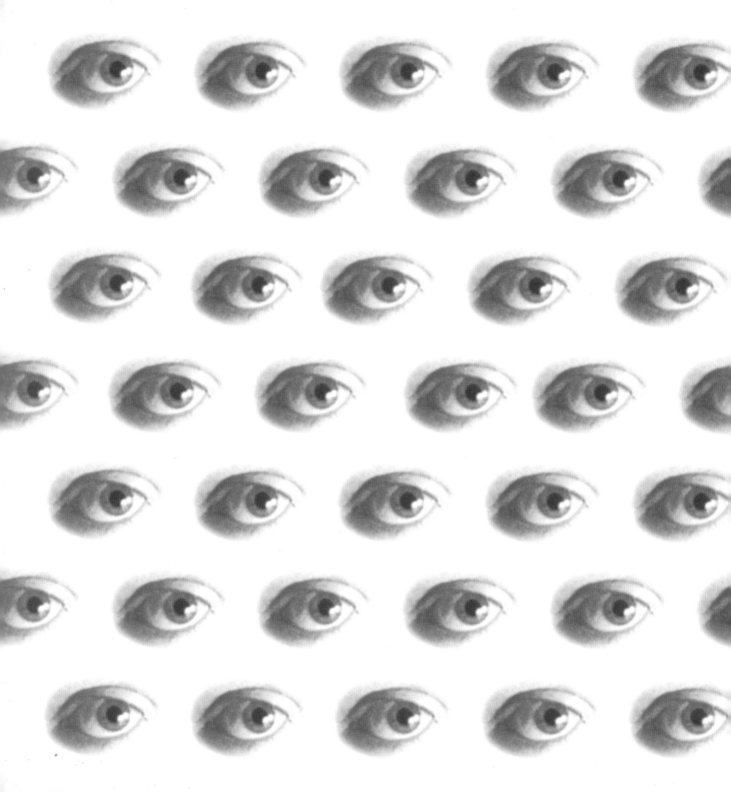